PREFACE

Professional skills and ethics are vital in shaping competent, ethical professionals equipped to navigate today's complex work environment. These subjects are integral to modern education, instilling in students the ability to act with integrity, responsibility, and sound judgment in their careers. Recognizing their importance, the Indira Gandhi National Open University (IGNOU) has made these topics a core part of its curriculum, pushing students to master both theoretical concepts and practical applications.

This book, *IGNOU MCA MCS 214 Professional Skills and Ethics Previous Year Solved Papers*, is a carefully curated compilation of unsolved question papers from previous years. It serves as an essential resource for students preparing for exams, helping them assess their understanding, identify weaknesses, and improve their problem-solving skills. Practicing with past papers is a proven method for effective exam preparation. It not only familiarizes students with the types and formats of questions but also deepens their understanding by applying concepts to practical scenarios. By working through these unsolved papers, students can gauge their exam readiness, enhance time management, and build confidence in tackling challenging questions.

The decision to leave these papers unsolved encourages active engagement, critical thinking, and exploration of multiple problem-solving approaches. This method fosters independent learning, better preparing students for the variety of questions they may face in exams. Covering a broad spectrum of topics—communication skills, leadership, workplace ethics, and legal considerations—this book provides thorough coverage of the syllabus, ensuring students grasp the essential concepts for exam success. We hope this book supports your academic journey and inspires deeper exploration into professional skills and ethics. The knowledge gained here will undoubtedly be invaluable in shaping your future career. Wishing you success in your studies and future endeavours in the professional world.

Table of Contents

MCS-214

MASTER IN COMPUTER APPLICATION (MCA) (NEW)

Term-End Examination

December, 2021

MCS-214: PROFESSIONAL SKILLS AND ETHICS

Time: 2 Hours

Maximum Marks: 50

Note: Answer all questions.

---

1. Read the following passage and answer the questions below it:

Once you've mastered reading the cues and emotions of other people, you're ready to read an entire room. It may sound daunting, but it's what you've already learned about social awareness—just on a larger scale.

Essentially, there are two ways to pick up the mood of an entire room. First, you can rely solely on your gut instincts. Emotions are contagious, meaning they spread from one or two people until there's a palpable and collective mood that you will feel at some level. For example, imagine walking into a room of 125 entrepreneurs who are networking and sharing their ideas. It's pretty likely that there would be excitement and positive energy there, and it wouldn't take long to become aware of it. You'd hear their voice levels and tones, and see the focused and interested posture and body language. Now imagine walking into a room of 125 people waiting to be chosen for jury duty

The room is quiet; people are trying to distract themselves with reading material, music, and anything else to pass the time. Even though it's our civic duty to attend, hardly anyone wants to be there. The two moods are like night and day. Here's how you can catch the mood of the room. When you enter the room, scan it and notice whether you feel and see energy or quiet, subdued calm. Take notice of how people are arranging themselves—alone or in groups. Are they talking and moving their hands? Are some more animated than others? What is your gut telling you about them?

Another way to read the mood of the room is to bring along a more experienced guide, much like you would on an African safari. Your guide should be a socially aware expert willing to show you the ropes when it comes to tapping into your instincts and picking up the room's mood. Shadow your guide and listen to what he feels and sees. Ask what he senses and what clues gave the mood away. Eventually, you should be in one to take the lead.

Questions:

1. (a) Answer the following questions:

(i) What do you think the author means by 'the mood of the room'? 2

Answer: The "mood of the room" refers to the overall emotional atmosphere or energy present in a group of people gathered in a space. It reflects the collective emotions, attitudes, and behaviours of the people in the room, which can be observed through their body language, tone of voice, and interactions.

(ii) Discuss the two ways to "pick up the mood of the room." Give examples. 2+2

Answer:

Relying on gut instincts: By observing body language, tone of voice, and posture, you can feel the collective mood. For example, in a room of 125 entrepreneurs, you would sense excitement and energy from their animated discussions.
Using a socially aware guide: An experienced person can help you recognize the mood by pointing out cues like facial expressions, group dynamics, or individual behaviours, similar to how a guide helps on a safari.

(iii) What does the author suggest that we should do to 'catch' the mood of the room?

2

Answer: The author suggests scanning the room and observing the energy, interactions, and body language of the people present. Noticing whether people are engaging in animated conversations or remaining quiet can help catch the mood. You can also bring along an experienced guide to help you read the mood by explaining the cues they notice.

(iv) Give a title to the passage and give reasons for it.

2

Answer:
Title: "Reading the Mood of a Room"
Reason: The passage explains how to perceive and interpret the overall emotional atmosphere of a group by observing body language, group dynamics, and emotions. The focus is on methods for understanding the collective mood, making this title appropriate.

(b) Find words/phrases from the passage which mean the same as the following: 6

i. Signs/prompts (para 1)

Answer: Cues

ii. Intimidating/frightening (para 1)

Answer: Daunting

iii. Ttransmittable (para 2)

Answer: Contagious

iv. Business person (para 2)

Answer: Entrepreneur

v. Instinctive feeling (para 3)

Answer: Gut instincts

vi. Evaluate the room (para 4)

Answer: Can the room

(c) Make sentences of your own with the following words/phrases from the passage: 4

(i) Emotions

Answer: The speaker's powerful words stirred strong emotions in the audience.

(ii) Networking

Answer: Networking events provide a great opportunity to meet potential business partners.

(iii) Distract

Answer: The noise from the construction site was enough to distract everyone in the office.

(iv) hone your ability

Answer: To excel in public speaking, you need to continuously hone your ability to communicate clearly.

2. Write short notes on any two of the following:

2x5=10

i. The qualities of a star performer

ii. Building self-confidence

iii. What constitutes plagiarism?

iv. Leading an ethical life both personally and

v. Professionally

Answer:

i. The qualities of a star performer: A star performer excels in their work due to several qualities: dedication, expertise, and adaptability. They consistently deliver high-quality results, often exceeding expectations. Strong communication skills, a positive attitude, and the ability to collaborate with others also distinguish them. Their ability to handle pressure and stay motivated ensures that they stand out in their professional environment.

ii. Building self-confidence: Building self-confidence involves self-awareness, developing skills, and facing challenges head-on. A confident person believes in their abilities, sets realistic goals, and maintains a positive mindset. Regular practice, preparation, and learning from experiences contribute to increasing self-assurance. Surrounding oneself with supportive people and celebrating small victories also play a vital role.

iii. What Constitutes Plagiarism? Plagiarism involves using someone else's work, ideas, or expressions without proper acknowledgment and presenting them as one's own. This can range from copying text, data, images, or music to paraphrasing someone's original concepts without citation. Plagiarism can occur in academic, artistic, and professional contexts and is considered unethical and, in many cases, a legal infringement. Avoiding plagiarism requires diligent citation and referencing of all sources and understanding and adhering to the specific requirements and standards set by educational institutions or professional fields.

iv. Leading an Ethical Life Personally: Leading an ethical life involves adhering to principles of integrity, honesty, fairness, and respect in personal interactions and decisions. It means being truthful and transparent with oneself and others, making decisions that do not harm others, and treating people with dignity. Personal ethics also involve taking responsibility for one's actions and their consequences, fostering a spirit of kindness and compassion, and striving for consistency between one's values and actions.

v. Leading an Ethical Life Professionally: In a professional context, leading an ethical life means maintaining professional integrity, confidentiality, and transparency in workplace dealings. It requires adherence to the laws and regulations governing one's profession and the ethical codes set by professional bodies. Ethical leadership involves treating colleagues, clients, and all professional contacts with respect and fairness, ensuring equitable treatment and opportunities. It also includes making decisions that not only promote personal and organizational success but also benefit the wider community and environment, reflecting a commitment to corporate social responsibility.

3. (i) Fill in the blanks with a/an, the or no article: **0.5 each**

The larger ____________ meeting, the more difficult it becomes to reach a _________ decision. _________ ideal size of _________ meeting depends on ________ purpose of __________ meeting. If _________ meeting has been called to take __________ decision on any matter, it is advisable to call just _________ few individuals for it. All __________ meetings have something in common.

Answer:

The larger ___*the*___ meeting, the more difficult it becomes to reach at ___*a*___ decision. ___*The*___ ideal size of ___*a*___ meeting depends on ___*the*___ purpose of ___*the*___ meeting. If ___*the*___ meeting has been called to take *a*___ decision on any matter, it is advisable to call just _______*an*_____ individual for it. All ______*the*______ meetings have something in common.

(ii) Rewrite the sentences below beginning with the words given below: **5**

a) The crop has been destroyed due to heavy rainfall.

Heavy rainfall ______________________

b) We will hold the meeting on the 10th of this month.

The meeting _______________________

c) The house is being sold.

They ___________________________

d) You are requested to maintain silence.

Please ________________________

e) The college has organized an inter- college debate competition.

An inter-college _____________________

Answer:

a) The crop has been destroyed due to heavy rainfall.

Heavy rainfall <u>has destroyed the crop.</u>

b) We will hold the meeting on the 10th of this month.

The meeting <u>will be held on the 10th of this month.</u>

c) The house is being sold.

They <u>are selling the house.</u>

d) You are requested to maintain silence.

Please maintain silence.

e) The college has organized an inter- college debate competition.

An inter-college debate competition has been organised by the college.

4. Write a letter to a friend about your new job in an IT company. Talk about: **10**

i. The work you do

ii. The satisfaction you derive from it

iii. Your supportive and friendly colleagues

You may use about **150** words.

Answer:

Dear Aayush,

I hope you're doing well! I'm excited to tell you about my new job at an IT company. I work as a software developer, focusing on creating web applications and ensuring the smooth functioning of our clients' systems. The work is both challenging and rewarding, as I get to solve complex problems and contribute to exciting projects.

What I love the most is the sense of satisfaction I get from my job. The company environment is great, and my colleagues are supportive and friendly. We often collaborate on tasks, and they are always willing to help out when needed. It's been an amazing experience so far, and I'm really enjoying my time here.

Hope to catch up soon!

Warm regards,

Arun

MCS-214

MASTER IN COMPUTER APPLICATION (MCA) (NEW)

Term-End Examination

June, 2022

MCS-214: PROFESSIONAL SKILLS AND ETHICS

Time: 2 Hours

Maximum Marks: 50

Note: Answer all questions.

---

1. Read the following passage and answer the questions below it:

20

Competition is a fact of life. To pretend that it doesn't exist or that you should avoid it all costs would be ridiculous. I've always loved to compete. As a child I was the fastest runner at school and the number one tennis player in Northern California in my age group. I was a high school All-American Athlete and went on to receive a college scholarship in tennis, where I played in the number one position and became the youngest captain in my team's history. I've run three marathons, one of them in three hours.

As an adult, my love of competition has continued, not only in sports, but in business as well. I love to negotiate, buy low, and sell high. I'm proud to be creative, and I'd like to believe I have a flair for marketing. The publishing world is fiercely competitive. I love to see my books doing well, and it's fun to get a standing ovation after a speech. I could certainly make the argument that if I didn't compete well, I wouldn't be helping very many people. So, it's important that I compete.

I tell you these things because I've spoken to many people who assume that I'm too relaxed to compete, which is not true. I don't want to give the impression, as I suggest you compete from the heart, that you can't compete effectively if you are a gentle person and become less attached to winning. You can have it all. You can be a winner and financially successful, have fun, compete hard, but never lose your perspective of what's most important—enjoying yourself, giving back, and taking it all in stride.

To compete from the heart means that you compete less from a desperate or neurotic need to achieve and more out of a love for what you do. Competing is its own reward. You are completely immersed in the process, absorbed

in the present moments of the activity— the business deal, the sale, the negotiation, interaction, or whatever. When you compete from your heart, the process itself provides the satisfaction; winning is secondary. When looked at in this healthier way, your business life becomes so much easier. You play hard—and then let go. You bounce back almost instantly.

You're resilient. You're a good sport. By not being so attached to a specific outcome (winning), you conserve energy and see hidden opportunities. You learn from your mistakes and losses. You move forward. Isn't it obvious that this not-so-attached attitude is in your best interest? It's been said, "Winning isn't everything, it's the only thing." To me, this is utter nonsense.

This philosophy stems from the fear that if you aren't consumed with winning, you never will win. I can tell you that I'm not consumed with winning—never have been, never will be—yet I've won many awards, contests, and first-place finishes. I've also done well

financially and made some wise investments. But none of my competitive accomplishments would mean anything to me if they weren't from the heart—
if I became so carried away with the competition and outcome that I forgot my humanity. So, to me, the "Winning is everything" motto is grossly inaccurate.

Questions:

(a) **(i)** What were the two things that the author excelled in, in his childhood? How did this benefit him? 2

Answer: The author excelled in running and tennis during his childhood. These achievements benefited him by providing him with recognition, such as being the fastest runner in school and the top tennis player in Northern California. His sports accomplishments also helped him secure a college scholarship in tennis, where he continued to excel and even became the youngest team captain.

(ii) What do you think is the author's profession(s)? Why? 2

Answer: The author seems to be involved in writing and public speaking. This can be inferred from the mention of his success in the publishing world, where his books do well, and he receives standing ovations after speeches. His love for marketing and negotiation also suggests a business-related profession.

(iii) Describe the "new" way of competing that the author suggests in para 3. 2

Answer: The "new" way of competing, according to the author, involves competing from the heart. This means competing out of love for the activity rather than from a neurotic need to win. The process itself becomes rewarding, and the focus shifts to enjoying the journey rather than obsessing over the outcome.

(iv) The author believes in "complete from the heart." What do you think this means? How is this philosophy different from "winning is everything"? Discuss. 4

Answer: Competing from the heart means participating in competitions because of a genuine passion and love for the activity itself, rather than a desperate need to win. The process of competition brings satisfaction, and the outcome, whether winning or losing, is secondary. This philosophy is different from "winning is everything," which focuses solely on achieving victory at any cost. The author suggests that the latter approach may lead to losing sight of one's humanity and personal growth, whereas competing from the heart emphasizes balance, enjoyment, and learning from both victories and losses.

(b) Find words/phrases from the passage which mean the same as the following: 5

i. Talent (para 2)

Answer: Flair

ii. Great applause (para 2)

Answer: Standing ovation

iii. To deal with a difficult situation in a calm way (para 3)

Answer: Taking it in stride

iv. Quick to recover (para 4)

Answer: Resilient

v. Totally preoccupied (para 5)

Answer: Consumed

(c) Make sentences with the following words/ phrases: 5

i. Marathons

Answer: Completing marathons requires immense physical endurance and mental strength

ii. Perspective

Answer: It's important to maintain perspective during challenging times to avoid getting overwhelmed.

iii. Neurotic

Answer: His neurotic need for perfection made it hard for him to enjoy his accomplishments.

iv. bounce back

Answer: After losing the game, she was determined to bounce back stronger in the next tournament.

v. Accomplishments

Answer: Her professional accomplishments include multiple awards for her innovative designs.

2. Write short notes on any two of the following:

$2\times5=10$

i. A brief history of copyright law
ii. Ethics at the workplace
iii. Personal and social competence
iv. What are "blind spots" and how to overcome them?
v. Collaboration and cooperation
vi. Presentation skills

Answer:

i. A brief history of copyright law:

Copyright law originated in the early 18th century with the introduction of the Statute of Anne in 1710 in England, which gave creators exclusive rights to their work for a limited time. Over time, copyright law has evolved globally to protect creators from unauthorized use of their intellectual property, including books, music, and software. Modern copyright laws provide protection for the lifetime of the author plus additional years after their death.

ii. Ethics at the workplace:

Workplace ethics refer to the moral principles and values that govern an individual's behaviour in a professional environment. Key components include honesty, accountability, fairness, respect, and integrity. Adhering to ethical practices ensures a positive work culture, fosters trust, and enhances professional relationships. Ethical workplaces also promote transparency and equality, which can lead to increased employee satisfaction and productivity.

iii. Personal and Social Competence: Personal and social competence encompasses a range of skills that allow individuals to manage themselves and their relationships effectively. Personal competence includes self-awareness, self-regulation, and motivation, crucial for understanding and managing one's emotions and behaviors. Social competence covers skills like empathy, effective communication, and conflict resolution, essential for interacting and building relationships with others. Developing these competences leads to better personal outcomes and stronger, more constructive social interactions.

iv. What are "Blind Spots" and How to Overcome Them? Blind spots in personal and professional contexts refer to the aspects of our personalities or behaviors that we are unaware of but are apparent to others. They can hinder personal growth and relationships. To overcome them, seek regular feedback from peers, mentors, or supervisors. Reflecting on this feedback, being open to criticism, and engaging in self-reflection are vital practices. Additionally, working with a coach or participating in workshops can provide insights and strategies for addressing blind spots effectively.

v. Collaboration and Cooperation: Collaboration and cooperation involve working jointly with others to achieve a common goal, emphasizing mutual benefit and collective success. Effective collaboration requires clear communication, shared objectives, and respect for diverse opinions and expertise. Cooperation, meanwhile, focuses on the supportive behaviors by individuals within the team to facilitate shared success. Both are critical in dynamic and diverse work environments, leading to innovative solutions and increased productivity.

vi. Presentation Skills: Presentation skills are crucial for effectively conveying information and engaging an audience. Key aspects include structuring content logically, making the material accessible and interesting, and using visual aids effectively. Good presenters also need to master public speaking skills, such as clear articulation, appropriate pacing, and confident body language. Additionally, adapting to feedback from the audience and handling questions competently are important to maintain engagement and deliver persuasive and impactful presentations.

3. (a) Fill in the blanks using the linking words given below: 5

There is one extra linker given:
yet, although, in spite of, unless, because, moreover

i. You can't take the exam _______________ you have 75% attendance.
ii. The building looks old ______________ it being maintained regularly.
iii. She couldn't reach on time _______________ the bus broke down on the way.
iv. She is not very resourceful ______________ she is always ready to help everyone.
v. ______________ he is quite old; he works very fast.

Answer:

i. You can't take the exam ___*unless*___ you have 75% attendance.

ii. The building looks old ___*in spite of*___ it being maintained regularly.

iii. She couldn't reach on time ___*because*__the bus broke down on the way.

iv. She is not very resourceful ___*yet*__ she is always ready to help everyone.

v. *Although*__ he is quite old, he works very fast.

4. Look at the following answers and form suitable questions: 5

i. Yes, I'll go with you.

Answer: Will you go with me?

ii. I met her at a party.

Answer: Where did you meet her?

iii. Of course, I can visit you tomorrow.

Answer: Can you visit me tomorrow?

iv. I suggest you exercise for 45 minutes every day.

Answer: What do you suggest I do every day?

v. No, it is not possible.

Answer: Is it possible?

5. You ordered for an I-pad on an online retailing service and you received a defective piece. Draft a letter to the head of Consumer Grievances of that organization indicating this and request for the replacement of the product. 10

Answer:

To

The Head of Consumer Grievances,

Technomad Online Retail,
1234 Innovation Avenue,
Metro City, 678900

Date: October 8, 2024

Subject: Request for Replacement of Defective iPad

Dear Sir/Madam,

I am writing to inform you that I recently purchased an iPad from your online retail platform (Order No. TNX987654321). Upon receiving the product, I discovered that it is defective. Specifically, the touchscreen is unresponsive, and the device frequently shuts down without warning.

I kindly request that you arrange for a replacement of the product at your earliest convenience. Please let me know the procedure for returning the defective unit and receiving the replacement. I look forward to your prompt assistance in this matter.

Thank you for your attention to this issue.

Yours sincerely,

Sashimi Verma
sashimi.verma@example.com
+91 98XXX XX210

MCS-214

MASTER IN COMPUTER APPLICATION (MCA) (NEW)

Term-End Examination

December, 2022

MCS-214: PROFESSIONAL SKILLS AND ETHICS

Time: 2 Hours

Maximum Marks: 50

Note: Answer all questions.

---

1. Read the following passage and answer the questions below it:

The world is often a dangerous place to do business in. For an organization to survive it must become adept at identifying and managing possible risks. In our personal lives we do this every day, often without thinking about it. Before we cross the road, we look around to make sure there isn't a vehicle heading towards us. And every parent weighs up all potential dangers before allowing their child to run the risk of riding a bike outside. Businesses have to make predicting, recognizing, and minimizing risk as natural and habitual as this. Some risks affect all businesses, such as the unpredictability of economics (e.g. inflation), politics (e.g. new legislation), and business realities (e.g. late payments). However, there are also risks specific to each sector. In the volatile telecommunications sector, a mobile phone company has to anticipate shifting customer taste in a market that is moving so fast it's hard to look one year into the future, let alone ten.

It's been said that the species most likely to survive is the one most responsive to change. The problem in risk assessment is that progression and change in today's world is no longer linear and predictable. The only successful business will be one that accepts uncertainty and is flexible enough to respond to change as it comes. That's where Watchman can help. This impressive software accepts a variety of inputs and then produces a stunning three-dimensional graphic display that allows you to view various risk factors at a glance, all against an interactive timeline. Intuitive controls allow you to filter the output to compare probabilities, determine the relative importance of each risk factor, and evaluate potential impact. And, of course, you can alter the variables to gauge how different conditions make an impact — in the hope that this knowledge will help you to avoid exposing your organization to unnecessary risks.

So, it's great as far as it goes, but there is a problem. If the input you provide is incomplete, this will affect the quality of the risk analysis. Watchman can't do the thinking for you and it can't determine whether a threat is directly relevant to your company. It is a sound program, but it is no replacement for the skilled, intuitive work done by an experienced risk manager.

Questions:

1. (a) Answer the following questions based on the passage:

i. What are the risks that all businesses face at some time or the other? 2

Answer: Businesses face risks such as economic unpredictability (e.g., inflation), political changes (e.g., new legislation), and business realities like late payments.

ii. What makes a business successful according to the passage?

2

Answer: A successful business is one that accepts uncertainty and is flexible enough to adapt to change. It must be responsive to change and ready to deal with unpredictable situations.

iii. What is 'Watchman' according to the passage? How does it help a business reduce its risk factors?

2

Answer: 'Watchman' is a software tool designed to help businesses manage risks. It uses various inputs to create a three-dimensional graphic display of risk factors, allowing users to compare probabilities, determine the importance of each risk, and evaluate the potential impact on the business. It helps by visualizing risks and providing insights to avoid unnecessary exposure.

iv. When does 'Watchman' not perform to its optimum? Why?

2

Answer: Watchman does not perform to its optimum when the input provided is incomplete. The software relies on accurate and complete data for its risk analysis. It cannot replace the intuitive and skilled work done by an experienced risk manager in identifying relevant threats.

v. Give an appropriate title to the passage and explain why it is appropriate.

2

Answer: "Managing Business Risks Effectively"**:** This title is appropriate because the passage discusses the importance of managing risks in business through prediction, analysis, and tools like Watchman. It also highlights how businesses must remain flexible and adaptive in a rapidly changing environment.

(b) Find words from the passage which mean the same as the following phrases/words: 5

i. Proficient/good at (para 1)

Answer: Adept

ii. Forecasting (para 1)

Answer: Predicting

iii. Changeable/ever-changing (para 2)

Answer: Volatile

iv. Instinctive (para 3)

Answer: Intuitive

v. To check out (para 3)

Answer: Evaluate

(c) Make sentences with the following words/phrases: 5

i. Survive

Answer: Only businesses that adapt to the market changes can survive in the long term.

ii. Minimizing

Answer: The company is focusing on minimizing production costs to stay competitive.

iii. Anticipate

Answer: The manager must anticipate customer demands to stay ahead of the competition.

iv. Stunning

Answer: The new advertising campaign received stunning feedback from the audience.

v. Evaluate

Answer: We need to evaluate all possible risks before launching the new product.

2. Write short notes on any two of the following:

10

i. Barriers to communication
ii. Characteristics and conventions of conversation
iii. How to be successful in a group discussion
iv. Qualities that employees must develop if they want to be successful
v. A brief history of Copyright

Answer:

i. Barriers to communication:

Barriers to communication are obstacles that hinder the effective exchange of information. These can include physical barriers (such as noise or distance), language differences, emotional or psychological barriers (like fear or stress), and cultural differences. Overcoming these barriers is essential for clear and successful communication. Using simple language, being a good listener, and ensuring that feedback is part of the communication process can help reduce these barriers.

ii. How to be successful in a group discussion:

Success in a group discussion depends on a variety of factors. Being well-prepared with knowledge on the topic, contributing thoughtfully, and listening actively are key. It's also important to communicate clearly, remain calm, and respect the opinions of others. Good body language and the ability to steer the discussion in a constructive direction can demonstrate leadership. Additionally, focusing on the group's objective and avoiding unnecessary arguments contribute to a positive outcome.

iii. How to be Successful in a Group Discussion:

Success in group discussions can be achieved by being well-prepared on the topic, listening actively, and contributing valuable insights. Effective participants are those who can articulate their thoughts clearly, respect different viewpoints, facilitate the involvement of quieter members, and help steer the group towards a constructive outcome. It is also important to avoid dominating the conversation and to use persuasive, not aggressive, communication.

iv. Qualities that Employees Must Develop if They Want to be Successful:

Employees aiming for success should develop a range of key qualities, including professionalism, adaptability, reliability, and teamwork skills. Other critical attributes include strong communication skills, problem-solving abilities, leadership qualities, and continuous learning and improvement. Employees who can demonstrate a strong work ethic and the ability to collaborate effectively with others typically excel in their careers.

v. A Brief History of Copyright:

Copyright is a legal mechanism used to protect the rights of creators over their intellectual property. The concept originated in the early 1700s in Britain with the Statute of Anne, which was the first copyright law granting authors rights over their printed works. The purpose was to encourage creativity and the dissemination of knowledge while providing economic benefits to authors. Over the centuries, copyright law has expanded globally and now covers a wide range of works including literature, music, software, and more, adapting to new technological advancements to protect creators' rights in the digital age.

3. **(a)** Write down the questions that led to each of these answers. The first one is done for you as an example.

5

i. Q: Are you Ms. Sen?

A: That's right. Pleased to meet you.

ii. Q: ______?

A: Yes thanks. I had a very good flight.

iii. Q: ______?

A: I would like to meet Mr. Prakash, if he's in the office.

iv. Q: ______?

A: No, my husband is travelling with me. I'm meeting him later.

v. Q: ______?

A: It was Mr. Jain who recommended the hotel to me.

Answer:

i. Q: Are you Ms. Sen?

A: That's right. Pleased to meet you.

ii. Q: <u>Did you have a good flight?</u>

A: Yes thanks. I had a very good flight.

iii. Q: <u>Whom would you like to meet?</u>

A: I would like to meet Mr. Prakash, if he's in the office.

iv. Q: <u>Are you travelling alone?</u>

A: No, my husband is travelling with me. I'm meeting him later.

v. Q: Who recommended the hotel to you?

A: It was Mr. Jain who recommended the hotel to me.

(b) Fill in the blanks with a/an, the or no article. 5

More and more ____________ shoppers are by-passing _____________ brand names for ___________ cheaper no-name products. This shows that even ___________ biggest and strongest brands in __________ world are vulnerable.

Answer:

More and more ___*the*___ shoppers are by-passing ___*the*___ brand names for ___*a*___ cheaper no-name products. This shows that even ___*the*___ biggest and strongest brands in ___*the*___ world are vulnerable.

2. Write a brief article in about 250 words on any one of the following topics: 10

i. Technology in the Classroom is the New Normal

ii. The World as a Global Village

iii. Protection of the Environment for the sake of the Future Generations

iv. The Impact of the Internet on Social Relations

v. AI in the Household.

Answer:

i. Technology in the Classroom is the New Normal

The integration of technology in educational settings has transformed traditional teaching methodologies, making digital tools the new norm in classrooms. This evolution enhances learning through interactive software, virtual experiments, and online resources that provide students with a more engaging and personalized learning experience. Tools like smartboards, tablets, and learning management systems allow for real-time feedback and foster an environment where students can learn at their own pace. As educators become more proficient in these technologies, the potential for shaping well-equipped future generations grows significantly.

(ii) The World as a Global Village

The world has become a global village due to advancements in communication and technology. Geographical barriers are no longer a hindrance, allowing people and businesses to interact and collaborate across continents instantly. Social media platforms, online businesses, and international news outlets enable people to share information and experiences with one another regardless of their physical location. This interconnectedness has fostered mutual understanding, cultural exchange, and global cooperation.

However, the global village also brings its challenges. While technology connects people, it can also create divisions based on economic inequality or political differences. Local cultures and identities sometimes struggle to maintain their uniqueness in the face of globalization. Despite these issues, the concept of a global village has empowered people to engage with each other on a scale never before imagined, offering opportunities for mutual growth and development.

This transformation has changed the way we live, work, and interact. With the right balance of innovation and respect for diversity, the global village can continue to offer benefits for future generations.

iii. Protection of the Environment for the Sake of Future Generations

Environmental protection is crucial for sustaining life on earth for future generations. This involves preserving natural habitats, conserving water, reducing pollution, and curbing the exploitation of natural resources. Sustainable practices and technologies, like renewable energy and waste recycling, are vital in mitigating environmental impacts. Educating the public about the effects of climate change and promoting policies that protect the environment are essential steps in ensuring a healthy planet for future inhabitants.

iv. The Impact of the Internet on Social Relations

The internet has profoundly influenced social relations, reshaping how people interact with one another. While it has enabled greater connectivity and the ability to maintain relationships across long distances, it has also led to new challenges such as digital isolation and a decline in face-to-face interactions. Social media, while facilitating connections, often promotes superficial interactions that can detract from more meaningful personal relationships. The impact of the internet is complex, affecting social dynamics and community structures around the world.

v. AI in the Household

Artificial Intelligence (AI) has made significant inroads into everyday household management, enhancing convenience and efficiency. Smart home devices, such as AI-powered thermostats, lighting systems, and security solutions, provide homeowners with unprecedented control over their living environments. AI assistants like Amazon Alexa or Google Home offer interactive experiences that assist with daily tasks, reminders, and entertainment, making AI an increasingly indispensable part of home life. As AI technology advances, its integration into household appliances and systems is set to revolutionize domestic routines.

MCS-214

MASTER IN COMPUTER APPLICATION (MCA) (NEW)

Term-End Examination

June, 2023

MCS-214: PROFESSIONAL SKILLS AND ETHICS

Time: 2 Hours

Maximum Marks: 50

Note: Answer all questions.

---

1. Read the following passage and answer the questions below it:

One of the greatest advances of modern technology has been the invention of computers. They are widely used in industries and universities. Now there is hardly any sphere of human life where computers have not been pressed into service of humans. We are heading fast towards a day when a computer will be as much a part of our daily life as a telephone or a computer. Computers are capable of doing extremely complicated work in all branches of learning. They can solve the most complex mathematical problems or put thousands of unrelated facts into order. These machines can be put to various uses. For instance, they can provide information in the best way to prevent traffic jams.

The process by which machines can be used to work for us has been called 'automation'. In the future, automation may enable human beings to enjoy more leisure than they do today. The coming of automation is bound to have important social consequences. Some years ago, an expert on automation, Sir Leon Bagrat pointed out that it was a mistake to believe that these machines could 'think'. There is no possibility that human beings will be 'controlled by machines.

Though computers are capable of learning from their mistakes and improving their performance, they need detailed instructions from human beings to operate. They can never, as it were, lead independent lives or 'rule the world' by making decisions on their own. Sir Leon said that in future, computers would be developed which would be small enough to carry in a pocket. Ordinary people would then be able to use them to obtain valuable information.

Computers could be plugged into a national network and be used like radios. For instance, people going on holiday could be informed about the weather conditions. Car drivers can be given alternative routes when there are traffic jams. It will also be possible to make tiny translating machines. This will enable people who do not share a common language to talk to each other without any difficulty.

Questions:

a. Answer the following questions:

5×2=10

i. Explain automation.

Answer: Automation refers to the process by which machines are used to perform tasks for humans. It allows for tasks to be completed efficiently without requiring continuous human intervention, potentially leading to more leisure time for people.

ii. Why can't computers lead independent lives or rule the world? Give two reasons.

Answer:

Computers need detailed instructions from humans to operate.

Although they can learn from mistakes, they cannot think or make independent decisions; they always require human input.

iii. What are Sir Leon's views on automation?

Answer: Sir Leon Bagrat believes that it is a mistake to think that computers can think independently or control humans. He asserts that even though computers may evolve and become more compact, they will always depend on human instruction and won't rule the world.

iv. Give the meaning of the following phrases:

'Controlled by machine'

'Rule the world'

Answer:

'Controlled by machine' – Being governed or directed by machines, where machines dictate actions instead of humans.

'Rule the world'– To dominate or have supreme control over global affairs or all aspects of life.

v. Give a suitable title to the passage and give reason for it.

Answer: Title: "The Role of Automation and Computers in Modern Society"

This title is appropriate because the passage discusses the role of computers and automation, highlighting their impact on society and how they are dependent on human input.

b. Find words or phrases from the passage that mean the some as following:

6

i. Make progress (Para 1)

Answer: Heading fast

ii. Creation (Para 1)

Answer: Invention

iii. Precious (Para 2)

Answer: Valuable

iv. Having the ability (Para 2)

Answer: Capable

v. Available as another possibility (Para 3)

Answer: Alternative

vi. A way or course (Para 3)

Answer: Route

c. Make sentences of your own with the following words/phrases from the passage: **4**

i. Widely

Answer: Artificial intelligence is widely used in various industries to improve efficiency.

ii. Complicated

Answer: The instructions for assembling the furniture were so complicated that I had to call for help.

iii. Possibility

Answer: There is a possibility that the event may be cancelled due to the weather.

iv. Conditions

Answer: The road conditions worsened after the heavy rains.

2. Write short notes on any two of the following in about 75 words each:

5×2=10

i. The qualities of a leader
ii. Problem solving skills
iii. Importance of feedback in communication
iv. Why is honesty the best policy?

Answer:

i. The qualities of a leader:

A leader possesses several qualities, including the ability to inspire and motivate others, excellent communication skills, empathy, and decision-making abilities. A good leader is also responsible, honest, and adaptable, capable of handling challenges with a calm demeanour.

ii. Problem-solving skills:

Problem-solving skills are essential for identifying issues, analysing them, and coming up with effective solutions. Critical thinking, creativity, and patience are vital components of problem-solving. It involves considering multiple perspectives and arriving at the best possible outcome.

iii. Importance of Feedback in Communication

Feedback is an integral part of effective communication, serving as a tool to improve and refine processes and performance in both professional and personal contexts. It helps in clarifying expectations, facilitating learning, and promoting personal and professional growth. Constructive feedback can reinforce positive behaviors and correct missteps, thereby enhancing efficiency and productivity. For feedback to be effective, it should be specific, timely, and delivered in a manner that is respectful and considerate. Receiving feedback well also requires openness and a willingness to engage in continuous improvement. Thus, feedback not only enhances communication but also strengthens relationships and fosters a culture of teamwork and development.

iv. Why is Honesty the Best Policy?

Honesty is celebrated as the best policy due to its profound impact on trust and reliability in relationships. Being honest promotes transparency and builds trust, which are foundational to strong and lasting personal and professional relationships. Honesty leads to fewer misunderstandings and conflicts because it ensures that communications are straightforward and clear. Additionally, living an honest life reduces stress, as it avoids the complications and anxieties associated with deceit. Moreover, honest individuals are often respected and valued in their communities, leading to better opportunities and more meaningful interactions. Ultimately, honesty fosters a sense of integrity and self-respect, making it a pivotal policy in achieving a fulfilling and uncomplicated life.

3. (i) Fill in the blanks with a, an, the or no article:

5

I am from Mumbai, Maharashtra. Mumbai is ___________ city in ___________ India. I live in ___________ house in __________ quiet street in ____________ countryside ___________ street is called 'Malad street' and ___________ house is more than 100 years old. I work as _____________ librarian at ____________ college near ___________ town.

Answer:

I am from Mumbai, Maharashtra. Mumbai is ____*a*____ city in ____*the*____ India. I live in _____*a*_____ house in ____*a*____ quiet street in ______*the*______ countryside *the*_____ street is called 'Malad street' and _____*the*_____ house is more than 100 years old. I work as _____*a*_____ librarian at _____*a*_____ college near _____*the*_____ town.

(ii). Rewrite the sentences beginning with the words given below:

5

i. The train has been delayed due to heavy floods.

Heavy floods ___________________________

ii. We will buy a car by next year.

A car _________________________________

iii. The game is played by them.

They __________________________________

iv. The parents requested the children to participate in Olympiad.

Please _________________________________

v. The University has launched a vocational course.

A vocational course _____________________

Answer:

i. The train has been delayed due to heavy floods.

Heavy floods have delayed the train.

ii. We will buy a car by next year.

A car will be bought by us by next year.

iii. The game is played by them.

They play the game.

iv. The parents requested the children to participate in Olympiad.

Please participate in the Olympiad, the parents requested the children.

v. The University has launched a vocational course.

A vocational course has been launched by the University.

4. Write a letter to your parents informing them about your internship at a Tech-firm HCL. Talk about: 10

i. Your work profile
ii. The incentives provided by workplace
iii. The challenges that you faced and overcome

You may use about **150** words.

Answer:

Rohit Verma
45/B, Green Park Society
Delhi, 110018
Date: October 8, 2024

Dear Mom and Dad,

I hope this letter finds you both in good health. I'm excited to let you know that I have secured an internship with HCL Technologies. My role here involves working on software development projects, troubleshooting various technical issues, and learning coding practices in real-world applications. The experience has been extremely rewarding, and I'm gaining valuable exposure to the IT industry.

The workplace environment is very supportive, and they've offered me a monthly stipend along with transportation benefits. One of the challenges I initially faced was working under tight deadlines, but I've managed to overcome this by improving my time management skills.

I'm looking forward to learning even more in the coming weeks and will keep you both updated on my progress.

Take care and talk to you soon.

Love,
Rohit

MCS-214

MASTER IN COMPUTER APPLICATION (MCA) (NEW)

Term-End Examination

December, 2023

MCS-214: PROFESSIONAL SKILLS AND ETHICS

Time: 2 Hours

Maximum Marks: 50

Note: Answer all questions.

---

1. Read the following passage and answer the questions below it:

Information Technology (IT) is the application of computers and internet to store, retrieve, transmit and manipulate information, often in the context of a business or other enterprise. IT is considered as a subset of Information and Communication Technology (ICT) and has evolved according to the needs. It is worth noting that the term IT is commonly used as a synonym for computers and it has, in this sense, shaped societies and adapted itself to people's needs. Humans were the first 'computers. Then machines were invented to carry out computational tasks. Now these machines have given way to a new form of information technology. Information has become accessible from anywhere through cloud technology. The term information technology in its modern sense first appeared in a 1958 article published in the Harvard Business Review; authors

Harold J. Leavitt and Thomas I. Whisler commented that the new technology does not yet have a single established name. We shall call it Information Technology (IT). Their definition consists of three categories: techniques for processing, the application of statistical and mathematical methods to decision-making and the simulation of higher-order thinking through computer programs and computer networks but it also encompasses other information distribution technologies such as television and telephones. Several industries are associated with information technology including computer hardware, software, electronics, semiconductors, internet, telecom equipment, engineering, health care, e-commerce, and computer services.

Thanks to the continuous development of computers, the original computing systems became minicomputers and later personal computers took the lead. Nowadays, mobile phones are dethroning the personal computer and computing is evolving faster to become disembodied like a cloud, becoming accessible more easily whenever needed. Information technology has transformed people and companies and has allowed digital technology to influence society and the economy alike.

Questions:

a. Answer the following questions:

5×2=10

i. Information technology is evolving mostly as a result of?

Answer: Information technology is evolving mostly due to advancements in computing systems, such as the development of minicomputers, personal computers, mobile devices, and cloud technology.

ii. The author claims that the first computers were?

Answer: The author claims that the first computers were humans, who performed computational tasks manually before machines were invented to automate these processes.

iii. What is the outcome of the development of information technology?

Answer: The outcome of the development of information technology is the transformation of society and businesses, making information easily accessible and allowing digital technology to influence social and economic aspects.

iv. What does it signify when computing systems take the shape of clouds?

Answer: When computing systems take the shape of clouds, it signifies that information and computing power are disembodied, stored remotely, and can be accessed easily from anywhere without the need for physical hardware.

v. Give a suitable title to the passage and give a reason for it.

Answer: A suitable title for the passage is "The Evolution and Impact of Information Technology." This title is appropriate because the passage discusses how IT has evolved over time and its profound impact on society and business.

b. Find words or phrases from the passage that mean the same as the following: 6

i. A place where items may be kept (Para 1)

Answer: Store

ii. To spend or convey from one person or place to another (Para 1)

Answer: Transmit

iii. Modify (Para 1)

Answer: Manipulate

iv. To create (Para 2)

Answer: Invented

v. A result or effect of an action or condition (Para 2)

Answer: Outcome

vi. Imitate (Para 2)

Answer: Simulation

c. Make sentences of your own with the following words from the passage: 4

i. Retrieve

Answer: I was able to retrieve all the lost files from the computer's backup system.

ii. Subset

Answer: Web development is a subset of Information Technology, focusing on building websites.

iii. Dethrone

Answer: Smartphones have dethroned personal computers as the primary device for internet access.

iv. Accessible

Answer: With cloud technology, information is accessible from anywhere with an internet connection.

2. Write short notes on any two of the following: **5×2=10**

i. Should anonymity be allowed on the internet?

ii. How important is time management?

iii. Your understanding of morality and ethics

iv. Impact of social media.

Answer:

i. Should anonymity be allowed on the internet?

Anonymity on the internet provides individuals the freedom to express their opinions without fear of retaliation. However, it also enables harmful behaviour like cyber bullying and misinformation. Striking a balance between protecting privacy and preventing abuse is crucial. Policies that allow anonymity with accountability may be necessary.

ii. How important is time management?

Time management is crucial for achieving success in both personal and professional life. Effective time management leads to increased productivity and efficiency, allowing for better project completion, stress reduction, and opportunities for advancement. It involves planning and executing tasks within set timelines, prioritizing work effectively, and setting goals that are attainable. Good time management also ensures a better balance between work and personal life, reducing the risk of burnout and improving overall well-being. Techniques like the use of calendars, to-do lists, and prioritization strategies can aid in developing strong time management skills. Ultimately, mastering time management enables individuals to make the most out of every day.

iii. Your Understanding of Morality and Ethics

Morality and ethics involve systems of beliefs and values that guide behavior and decisions in various cultural, religious, and personal contexts. Morality refers to the principles concerning the distinction between right and wrong or good and bad behavior, typically based on cultural or personal beliefs. Ethics, often used interchangeably with morality, specifically pertains to the rules provided by an external source, such as codes of conduct in workplaces or principles in professions. Both play a crucial role in societal functioning by maintaining standards of behavior that respect the rights and wellbeing of all individuals. Understanding and adhering to these principles are essential for fostering trust, cooperation, and harmony in interpersonal and societal interactions.

iv. Impact of Social Media

Social media has significantly impacted modern communication, reshaping how people connect, share information, and influence each other. Its benefits include fostering relationships, promoting awareness on various issues, and supporting business and marketing initiatives. However, social media can also contribute to negative outcomes such as misinformation, privacy breaches, and mental health issues like anxiety and depression. The platforms can create echo chambers, where users are exposed primarily to viewpoints similar to their own, which can polarize public opinion. Despite its challenges, social media's role in today's digital age is undeniably profound, offering tools for significant societal and personal influence and change. Effective management and responsible use are key to maximizing its benefits while minimizing harm.

3. (a) Fill in the blanks with a, an, the, or no article:

10×1/2=5

To say education is important is ____________ understatement. It is _____________ weapon to improve one's life. It is probably ______ most important to bring about social change. Education for _______________ child begins at home. It is ______ lifelong process that ends with death. Education certainly determines _____________ quality of _____________ individual's life. Education improves one's knowledge skill and develops ____________ personality and attitude most noteworthy. Education affects _______________ chance of employment for people. A highly educated individual is probably very likely to get ____________ good job.

Answer:

To say education is important is ___*an*___ understatement. It is ___*a*___ weapon to improve one's life. It is probably ___*the*___ most important to bring about social change. Education for ___*a*___ child begins at home. It is ___*a*___ lifelong process that ends with death. Education certainly determines ___*the*___ quality of *an*_____ individual's life. Education improves one's knowledge skill and develops *a*___ personality and attitude most noteworthy. Education affects ___*the*___ chance of employment for people. A highly educated individual is probably very likely to get *a*_____ good job.

(b) Rewrite the following sentences beginning with the word given below:

5

i. The girl has been feeling sick because of the weather.

Bad weather …

ii. I will write a book in the next semester.

A book …

iii. Your food is being prepared by him.

He is …

iv. You are requested to throw garbage in the dustbin.

Please …

v. She has stitched a new uniform for her sister.

A new uniform …

Answer:

i. The girl has been feeling sick because of the weather.

Bad weather <u>has been making the girl feel sick.</u>

ii. I will write a book in the next semester.

A book <u>will be written by me in the next semester.</u>

iii. Your food is being prepared by him.

He is <u>preparing your food.</u>

iv. You are requested to throw garbage in the dustbin.

Please <u>throw the garbage in the dustbin.</u>

v. She has stitched a new uniform for her sister.

A new uniform <u>has been stitched by her for her sister.</u>

4. Write a letter to your friend sharing details of a newly offered course in your university.

10

Talk about:

i. How innovative and different this course

ii. Your ideas and understanding about the course

iii. The scope of the course

You may use about **150** words.

Answer:

Rohit Verma

13/2709 MS Villa

Delhi, 110018

October 8, 2024

Dear Savita,

I hope this letter finds you in great spirits! I wanted to share some exciting news from our university. We have recently introduced a new course in Artificial Intelligence and Data Science, and I think it's something you would find fascinating.

This course is quite innovative, combining elements of AI, machine learning, and big data analytics. It focuses on practical skills in data handling and programming, which are essential for addressing real-world challenges. Given the rapid growth in these fields, this course has fantastic prospects in industries such as healthcare, finance, and technology

I truly believe this will open up a wealth of opportunities for us in the future. I'm eager to dive into this subject and would love to hear your thoughts about it!

Take care and keep in touch.

Best,

Rohit Verma

National Institute of Technology (NIT) Allahabad

MCS-214

MASTER IN COMPUTER APPLICATION (MCA)

Term-End Examination
June, 2022

MCS-214: PROFESSIONAL SKILLS AND ETHICS

Time: 2 Hours

Maximum Marks: 50

Note: Answer all questions.

---

1. Read the following passage and answer the questions below it:

Success in professional settings often depends on one's ability to work effectively within a team. While individual skills are essential, collaboration and communication play equally significant roles. In today's workplaces, diversity in perspectives, backgrounds, and skill sets can both enrich a team's approach and challenge its unity. Team members who excel in interpersonal skills are often those who actively listen, respect differing viewpoints, and demonstrate empathy toward their colleagues. However, conflicts are inevitable, particularly in high-stakes environments. The key to managing such situations lies in addressing issues openly and respectfully, focusing on shared goals rather than individual disagreements.

Consider, for instance, a scenario where team members disagree on a project deadline. An effective approach would involve listening to each party's concerns and finding a compromise that accommodates everyone's needs while still meeting project objectives. On the other hand, ignoring conflicts or prioritizing personal gain over team success can disrupt progress and harm morale. Leadership often means setting an example for conflict resolution and fostering a culture of mutual respect. Developing these professional skills is not only beneficial for team dynamics but also for personal growth and career advancement.

Questions:

a. What qualities does the author suggest are crucial for working effectively in a team?

2

Answer: The author suggests that collaboration, communication, interpersonal skills such as active listening, respecting differing viewpoints, and demonstrating empathy are crucial for working effectively within a team.

b. Why is conflict inevitable in team settings, and how can it be managed productively? Provide examples.

2

Answer: Conflict is inevitable in team settings due to diversity in perspectives, backgrounds, and skill sets which can lead to disagreements. Productive management of conflicts involves open and respectful discussion of issues, focusing on shared goals rather than personal disagreements. For example, if team members disagree on a project deadline, an effective resolution would involve listening to each person's concerns and finding a compromise that satisfies all parties while still achieving the project's objectives.

c. According to the passage, how can leadership impact team dynamics during conflicts? 2

Answer: Leadership impacts team dynamics during conflicts by setting an example for conflict resolution and fostering a culture of mutual respect. Effective leaders actively participate in conflict resolution, demonstrating how to address issues constructively and prioritize the team's success over individual gains.

d. Propose a suitable title for the passage and explain your choice. 2

Answer: "Mastering Team Dynamics for Effective Collaboration" - This title reflects the central theme of the passage, which emphasizes the importance of mastering interpersonal and leadership skills to enhance team collaboration and manage conflicts effectively.

e. Find words/phrases in the passage that mean the same as the following: 6

i. listening attentively (paragraph 1)

Answer: actively listen

ii. viewpoint (paragraph 1)

Answer: differing viewpoints

iii. solve or address (paragraph 2)

Answer: managing

iv. feelings of trust and well-being (paragraph 2)

Answer: morale

v. setting an example (paragraph 3)

Answer: setting an example for conflict resolution

b) Construct sentences using the following terms from the passage: 4

i. Collaboration

Answer: Effective collaboration among team members can significantly accelerate project timelines.

ii. Diversity

Answer: The diversity in our team's background brings a rich array of perspectives to the table, enhancing our problem-solving capabilities.

iii. Compromise

Answer: Finding a compromise is essential when team members have conflicting schedules but need to meet a common deadline.

iv. Leadership

Answer: Good leadership is not about asserting authority but about empowering each team member to perform at their best.

2. Write short notes on any two of the following: 5

   i. The traits of an effective communicator
   ii. Methods to enhance self-discipline in professional settings
   iii. Ethical decision-making in workplace conflicts
   iv. Balancing personal and professional responsibilities

Answer:

i. The traits of an effective communicator:

An effective communicator is clear, concise, and articulate. They ensure that their message is understood by adapting their communication style to their audience. They are also good listeners, which enables them to understand others' viewpoints and respond appropriately. Furthermore, an effective communicator is empathetic and can gauge the emotional context of their conversation, allowing for more effective interactions.

ii. Methods to Enhance Self-Discipline in Professional Settings

Enhancing self-discipline in the workplace can lead to increased productivity and better career advancement. Some methods to strengthen self-discipline include:

Set Clear Goals: Define specific, measurable, and realistic goals that provide direction and a sense of purpose.

Create a Structured Schedule: Plan daily tasks and adhere to a routine that optimizes productivity while including short breaks to prevent burnout.

Use Time Management Tools: Implement tools and apps that track time spent on tasks, helping to focus and manage time effectively.

Limit Distractions: Identify workplace distractions and create strategies to minimize them, such as setting boundaries with coworkers or using noise-cancelling headphones.

Self-Monitor and Reflect: Regularly review your work and behavior to self-assess and adjust actions accordingly.

Build Healthy Habits: Strengthen discipline through consistent daily habits that support work tasks and personal well-being.

iii. Ethical decision-making in workplace conflicts:

Ethical decision-making in workplace conflicts involves making choices that are fair, just, and impartial while considering the well-being of all parties involved. It requires transparency, where all stakeholders understand the reasoning behind decisions. It also demands accountability, where decision-makers are responsible for the outcomes of their actions, ensuring that decisions adhere to both organizational values and legal standards.

iv. Balancing Personal and Professional Responsibilities

Balancing personal and professional life is crucial for maintaining overall well-being and job satisfaction. Effective strategies include:

Prioritize Tasks: Evaluate the importance of various tasks and prioritize them to ensure that key responsibilities in both areas are met.

Set Boundaries: Establish clear boundaries between work and personal life, such as specific work hours and dedicated family time.

Learn to Delegate: At work and at home, delegate tasks when possible to relieve pressure and engage others in responsibilities.

Use Technology Wisely: Utilize technology to streamline tasks but also ensure it does not invade personal time.

Take Time Off: Regular breaks and vacations can rejuvenate one's mind and body, improving efficiency and focus when returning to work.

Communicate Needs: Openly communicate needs and challenges with employers, family, and friends to receive support and understanding.

3. Grammar and Transformation Exercises:

a. Fill in the blanks with *a*, *an*, *the*, or no article:

0.5 each

i. As __________ member of __________ team, you must be aware of __________ team's goals.

ii. Diversity in __________ workplace is essential for __________ innovation.

iii. Being __________ empathetic leader is __________ key to earning respect.

iv. One of __________ most important traits of __________ successful professional is adaptability.

Answer:

i. As **a** member of **a** team, you must be aware of **the** team's goals.

ii. Diversity in **the** workplace is essential for **the** innovation.

iii. Being **an** empathetic leader is **the** key to earning respect.

iv. One of **the** most important traits of **a** successful professional is adaptability.

b. Rewrite the sentences below beginning with the words given below:

5

i. They offered incentives to improve employee productivity.

Begin with: …………………

ii. The management team resolved the conflict.

Begin with: ………………………

iii. The employees are asked to attend a training session.

Begin with: ……………………..

iv. She is creating a report on workplace ethics.

Begin with: …………………

v. The HR team organized an orientation program.

Begin with: ……………………..…

Answer:

i. They offered incentives to improve employee productivity.

Begin with: Incentives to improve employee productivity were offered.

ii. The management team resolved the conflict.

Begin with: The conflict was resolved by the management team.

iii. The employees are asked to attend a training session.

Begin with: A training session is to be attended by the employees.

iv. She is creating a report on workplace ethics.

Begin with: A report on workplace ethics is being created by her.

v. The HR team organized an orientation program.

Begin with: An orientation program was organized by the HR team.

4. Letter Writing: (10 marks)

Write a letter to a friend describing your experience working on a recent team project. Discuss:

The nature of the project and your responsibilities

Challenges faced and how they were managed

Lessons learned from collaborating with the team

Answer in approximately 150 words.

Answer:

To: Ria

From: Rani

Subject: Reflecting on My Recent Team Project Experience

Dear Ria,

I hope this letter finds you well. I recently completed a challenging yet rewarding team project at work, and I thought to share some insights from that experience with you.

Our project aimed to develop a new software tool designed to enhance data security within our company. As a project manager, I was responsible for overseeing the development process, coordinating between different departments, and ensuring that all project milestones were met on time.

One of the major challenges we faced was aligning the diverse perspectives and expertise of team members to meet the project's complex requirements. However, through open communication and regular strategy meetings, we were able to address these challenges effectively. We also encountered a few technical glitches that required quick thinking and collaboration to resolve.

This project taught me the importance of patience and flexibility in teamwork. I learned that effective collaboration requires understanding and adapting to different working styles and that these challenges are opportunities for growth.

Thank you for taking the time to read about my experience. I look forward to hearing from you soon and learning about your recent endeavors as well.

Warm regards,
Rani

Anna University, Chennai

MCS-214

MASTER IN COMPUTER APPLICATION (MCA)

Term-End Examination
June, 2021

MCS-214: PROFESSIONAL SKILLS AND ETHICS

Time: 2 Hours

Maximum Marks: 50

Note: Answer all questions.

---

1. Read the following passage and answer the questions below it:

Professionalism in today's workplaces extends far beyond technical skills and knowledge. It involves maintaining ethical standards, building trust, and fostering respectful interactions. Professional ethics guide how employees interact with others, make decisions, and manage information. Confidentiality is one of the pillars of ethical conduct. In any profession, employees are often entrusted with sensitive information about clients, colleagues, or the company. Misuse of such information can damage reputations and erode trust. For instance, healthcare providers must safeguard patient records, while finance professionals are responsible for securing clients' financial data.

Another crucial aspect of professionalism is transparency, which allows organizations to cultivate trust and open communication. When leaders are transparent about changes or challenges, employees are better prepared to adapt. Transparency, however, needs to be practiced with discretion, ensuring that shared information remains relevant and respectful. Conflicts of interest can also impact workplace ethics. Personal interests that clash with professional responsibilities create bias and can undermine fairness in decision-making. Managing such conflicts is crucial to maintaining integrity and impartiality. Ethical workplaces foster a culture of respect, accountability, and teamwork, benefiting both employees and the organization.

When ethics, transparency, and respect are prioritized, the result is a workplace that promotes growth, innovation, and mutual trust. Professionalism not only leads to a productive work culture but also contributes to the long-term success of the organization.

Questions:

a. Answer the following questions:

i. Explain the role of confidentiality in maintaining professional ethics. Give an example. 2

Answer: Confidentiality in professional ethics involves safeguarding sensitive information provided by clients, colleagues, or the organization. It is essential for maintaining trust and integrity within professional relationships. For example, in the healthcare sector, providers are required to maintain the confidentiality of patient records to protect their privacy and personal health information, thus upholding the ethical standards of the medical profession.

ii. What is the importance of transparency in an organization, according to the passage? 2

Answer: Transparency is crucial in organizations as it cultivates trust and open communication. By being transparent about changes and challenges, organizations enable employees to better adapt to new situations. This openness leads to a more informed and cohesive workforce, which can navigate challenges more effectively.

iii. Describe how conflicts of interest affect workplace ethics. 2

Answer: Conflicts of interest can severely impact workplace ethics by creating bias and undermining fairness in decision-making. When personal interests conflict with professional responsibilities, it can lead to decisions that are not in the best interest of the organization or its clients, thereby damaging the ethical fabric of the workplace.

iv. Based on the passage, why is it important to practice transparency with discretion? 2

Answer: Practicing transparency with discretion is important because it ensures that the information being shared is relevant and respectful. While openness is beneficial, indiscriminate sharing can lead to issues like information overload or breaches of privacy. Discretion helps in maintaining professionalism and ensures that transparency does not compromise sensitive information.

v. What are the key outcomes of prioritizing ethics, respect, and transparency in the workplace? 2

Answer: Prioritizing ethics, respect, and transparency leads to a workplace that promotes growth, innovation, and mutual trust. This environment encourages a productive work culture and contributes to the long-term success of the organization by fostering accountability, teamwork, and a respectful atmosphere.

b. Provide words/phrases from the passage which mean the same as:

Essential principle (para 1)

Answer: pillars

Responsible for managing (para 1)

Answer: are responsible for

Openness (para 2)

Answer: transparency

Clash (para 3)

Answer: conflicts of interest

Responsibility (para 3)

Answer: professional responsibilities

Promote (para 4)

Answer: fosters

c) Make sentences of your own with the following words/phrases from the passage:

(4 marks)

i. Confidentiality

Answer: Confidentiality is a cornerstone of trust between a lawyer and their client.

ii. Integrity

Answer: The integrity of the auditor ensures that financial reports are free from bias and inaccuracies.

iii. Bias

Answer: To avoid bias in hiring, the company implemented a new blind recruitment process.

iv. Teamwork

Answer: Teamwork in the workplace can lead to greater efficiency and a happier work environment.

2. Write short notes on any two of the following:

5 each

(i) Characteristics of a trustworthy employee
(ii) Building confidence in a professional setting
(iii) The importance of transparency in leadership

Answer:

(i) Characteristics of a trustworthy employee:

A trustworthy employee is reliable, honest, and ethical in all their professional dealings. They consistently meet deadlines, keep their promises, and are counted on in critical situations. Moreover, such employees handle confidential information with care and respect the privacy of their colleagues and clients.

(ii) Building confidence in a professional setting:

Building confidence in a professional setting involves developing competence, communicating effectively, and receiving constructive feedback. Confidence can be enhanced by setting and achieving small goals, mentoring others, and engaging in continuous professional development.

(iii) The importance of transparency in leadership:

Transparency in leadership is vital for building trust, fostering open communication, and creating a loyal team. Transparent leaders share important information with their team, involve them in decision-making, and openly discuss the organization's challenges and successes, which encourages a shared sense of purpose and commitment.

3. Grammar Exercises 5 each

a) Fill in the blanks with a/an, the, or no article:

Purpose of __________ meeting is to create an open forum where _________ participants feel comfortable sharing their thoughts. In _________ ethical workplace, employees are valued and feel _________ part of __________ team. Leaders should ensure that ___________ environment is respectful and supportive.

Answer:

Purpose of **the** meeting is to create an open forum where **the** participants feel comfortable sharing their thoughts. In **an** ethical workplace, employees are valued and feel **part** of **the** team. Leaders should ensure that **the** environment is respectful and supportive.

b) Rewrite the sentences below beginning with the words given below:

(i) Ethical workplaces promote mutual respect among team members.

Mutual respect among team members _________.

(ii) Teamwork enhances productivity in the office.

Productivity in the office _________.

(iii) Professionalism can make a positive impact on career growth.

Career growth _________.

(iv) The company upholds high standards of integrity.

High standards of integrity _________.

(v) Confidentiality is crucial in many professions.

Many professions _________.

Answer:

i. Ethical workplaces promote mutual respect among team members.

Mutual respect among team members is promoted by ethical workplaces.

ii. Teamwork enhances productivity in the office.

Productivity in the office is enhanced by teamwork.

iii. Professionalism can make a positive impact on career growth.

Career growth can be positively impacted by professionalism.

iv. The company upholds high standards of integrity.

High standards of integrity are upheld by the company.

v. Confidentiality is crucial in many professions.

Many professions consider confidentiality crucial.

4. Write a letter to a friend about a professional development workshop you attended. Describe: 10

Key learnings from the workshop

How it has impacted your professional skills

Why you would recommend it

(Use approximately 150 words)

Answer:

To: Ria

From: Rani

Subject: Updates on professional development workshop

Dear Ria,

I hope this letter finds you well. I recently attended a professional development workshop focused on "Emerging Trends in Digital Marketing," and I must tell you, it was enlightening!

The workshop covered various topics such as SEO, content marketing, and data analytics. The insights provided by industry experts have greatly enhanced my understanding of the digital landscape, and I've already started applying some of the strategies at work.

One of the key learnings was about the importance of personalizing marketing content to enhance customer engagement. The practical sessions on analytics tools were particularly impactful, helping me to better analyze consumer behavior and preferences.

I highly recommend attending such workshops as they not only boost your skills but also keep you updated with industry trends. It's definitely a worthwhile investment for personal and professional growth.

Looking forward to catching up soon and hearing about your own professional endeavors.

With Regards
Your Rani

Vellore Institute of Technology (VIT), Vellore

MCS-204

MASTER IN COMPUTER APPLICATION (MCA)

Term-End Examination

June, 2022

MCS-204: PROFESSIONAL SKILLS AND ETHICS

Time: 2 Hours

Maximum Marks: 50

Note: Answer all questions.

---

1. Read the following passage and answer the questions below it:

In today's fast-paced professional world, the importance of ethical decision-making and integrity has gained significant attention. Ethics serve as the foundation of professional behaviour and trust within workplaces. While technical skills are necessary, they alone are not sufficient for long-term success. Professionalism encompasses both competence in one's field and adherence to ethical principles.

Ethics in the workplace often revolves around honesty, respect, fairness, and accountability. Employees are expected to handle sensitive information discreetly, fostering an environment of trust. Confidentiality, as an ethical principle, requires that private information be safeguarded and not used for personal advantage. This is especially relevant in professions such as law, healthcare, and finance, where clients' sensitive information is entrusted to professionals who must maintain strict confidentiality. Additionally, ethical behaviour extends to being transparent in communication, acknowledging one's mistakes, and taking responsibility for actions.

One crucial aspect of professionalism is the ability to manage conflicts of interest. Conflicts can arise when personal motives clash with professional responsibilities. In such cases, impartiality becomes essential, and employees should avoid making decisions that could be perceived as biased or unfair. This builds a culture of fairness and reliability within an organization.

Furthermore, ethical leadership sets the tone for organizational culture. Leaders who prioritize integrity, transparency, and accountability foster a supportive environment that encourages employees to adopt similar values. When leaders openly communicate decisions, share organizational goals, and admit to errors, they model the behaviour expected within the organization. This transparency also allows employees to engage in open dialogue, promoting innovation and collaboration.

Ethics and professionalism also contribute to an organization's reputation. A company known for its ethical practices is more likely to gain the trust of its clients and the public, leading to sustained growth and profitability. For instance, organizations that prioritize environmentally responsible practices not only reduce their ecological impact but also build a positive public image. Customers and investors often prefer companies that align with ethical values, showing that integrity in business is not only the right choice but also a strategic one.

In conclusion, professionalism and ethics are interlinked pillars that support a productive and trustworthy workplace. By upholding ethical standards, employees and leaders alike can contribute to a work environment that values respect, accountability, and growth. Ethical behaviour, when ingrained in an organization's culture, can lead to lasting success and mutual respect between the organization and its stakeholders.

Questions:

a. Answer the following questions:

i. Explain the role of confidentiality in professional ethics, as mentioned in the passage. 2

Answer: Confidentiality in professional ethics involves the responsibility to safeguard and not misuse private information entrusted by clients or pertaining to the company. It is critical in maintaining trust and integrity in professions such as law, healthcare, and finance, where sensitive information must be protected from unauthorized disclosure.

ii. How does managing conflicts of interest contribute to workplace fairness? 2

Answer: Managing conflicts of interest contributes to workplace fairness by ensuring decisions are made impartially and without bias. When personal motives do not clash with professional responsibilities, decisions made are fair and perceived as just by all stakeholders, thereby fostering a culture of reliability and ethical integrity within the organization.

iii. What role does ethical leadership play in shaping organizational culture? Provide examples from the passage. 2

Answer: Ethical leadership plays a pivotal role in shaping organizational culture by prioritizing integrity, transparency, and accountability. Leaders who openly communicate decisions, admit errors, and share organizational goals model behavior that promotes a supportive environment. This, in turn, encourages employees to adopt similar values, fostering innovation and collaboration, as demonstrated when leaders model admitting to errors and sharing decisions.

iv. According to the passage, how can ethical practices impact a company's public image? 2

Answer: Ethical practices can significantly enhance a company's public image by building trust with clients and the public. Organizations known for ethical behaviors, such as prioritizing environmentally responsible practices, attract customers and investors who value these qualities, thereby not only doing the right thing but also gaining a competitive edge in the market.

v. What are the benefits of promoting ethics and professionalism in the workplace? 2

Answer: Promoting ethics and professionalism in the workplace leads to a productive and trustworthy environment that values respect, accountability, and growth. It contributes to the organization's reputation, aids in attracting and retaining talent, and ensures sustained growth and profitability by fostering a positive public image and customer loyalty.

b. Find words/phrases from the passage which mean the following: 6

Fundamental basis (para 1)

Answer: foundation

Secure and protect (para 2)

Answer: safeguarded

Neutrality (para 3)

Answer: impartiality

Authority figures (para 4)

Answer: Leaders

Collective success (para 5)

Answer: mutual respect between the organization and its stakeholders

Long-lasting (para 6)

Answer: lasting success

c. Create sentences of your own using the following words/phrases from the passage: (4 marks)

Transparency

Answer: In our department, transparency in how decisions are made has significantly increased team trust.

Collaboration

Answer: The collaboration between the marketing and sales teams led to a highly successful product launch.

Reputation

Answer: Our company's reputation for excellent customer service has contributed to its market leadership.

Mutual respect

Answer: Mutual respect is essential for fostering a productive and harmonious workplace.

2. Write short notes on any two of the following: 5 each

a) The impact of ethical behaviour on career progression
b) The role of transparency in organizational success
c) Building trust in professional relationships

Answer:

a) The impact of ethical behavior on career progression

Ethical behavior positively impacts career progression by building a professional's reputation for reliability and integrity. It leads to higher trust from management and colleagues, often resulting in promotions and leadership opportunities. Ethical individuals are seen as role models and are more likely to be given responsibilities that require a high degree of trust and discretion.

b) The role of transparency in organizational success

Transparency is crucial in organizational success as it fosters an open and honest work environment. It helps in managing expectations, facilitating better decision-making, and enhancing employee morale. Transparent practices ensure that all members of the organization are aligned with its goals and have a clear understanding of how their roles contribute to overall success.

c) Building trust in professional relationships

Building trust in professional relationships requires consistency, honesty, and open communication. It involves delivering on promises, showing respect for others' opinions, and acting with integrity even in difficult situations. Trust is foundational in professional relationships as it leads to more effective collaboration and communication, essential for achieving personal and organizational goals.

3. Grammar Exercises

a. Fill in the blanks with a/an, the, or no article:

0.5 each

_____ organization known for _______ ethical practices is more likely to gain _______ trust of _______ clients. In _______ fast-paced world of business, _______ companies that prioritize ethics and accountability find long-term success.

Answer:

An organization known for ethical practices is more likely to gain the trust of clients. In the fast-paced world of business, companies that prioritize ethics and accountability find long-term success.

b. Rewrite the sentences below beginning with the words given below: (5 marks)

i. Ethical companies often retain loyal customers.

Loyal customers _________.

ii. Professionalism enhances workplace trust.

Workplace trust _________.

iii. Organizations prioritize transparency to foster a positive culture.

A positive culture _________.

iv. Employees should avoid conflicts of interest.

Conflicts of interest _________.

v. Maintaining confidentiality is crucial in healthcare.

In healthcare, _________.

Answer:

i. Ethical companies often retain loyal customers.

Loyal customers <u>are often retained by ethical companies.</u>

ii. Professionalism enhances workplace trust.

Workplace trust <u>is enhanced by professionalism.</u>

iii. Organizations prioritize transparency to foster a positive culture.

A positive culture <u>is fostered by organizations that prioritize transparency.</u>

iv. Employees should avoid conflicts of interest.

Conflicts of interest <u>should be avoided by employees.</u>

v. Maintaining confidentiality is crucial in healthcare.

In healthcare, <u>maintaining confidentiality is crucial.</u>

4. Write a letter to a colleague about an upcoming ethics workshop in your organization. Discuss: (10 marks)

The topics that will be covered

Why attending it would be beneficial

How it aligns with the organization's values

(Use approximately 150 words)

Answer:

Dear Raj,

I hope this message finds you well. I am writing to inform you about an upcoming professional development opportunity that I believe will be greatly beneficial to us and our team. We are hosting an Ethics Workshop next month, focusing on "Ethical Decision Making in a Modern Corporate Environment."

The workshop will cover several vital topics, including navigating ethical dilemmas, fostering an inclusive workplace, and the importance of maintaining integrity in our day-to-day operations. These sessions will be led by respected leaders in the field and are designed to equip us with practical tools and insights that can be directly applied to our roles.

Attending this workshop will not only enhance our skills in making well-considered decisions but also align perfectly with our organization's values of transparency, responsibility, and respect. The knowledge gained here will undoubtedly contribute to our professional growth and the ethical culture of our company.

Furthermore, embracing the principles discussed can help us lead by example and influence our colleagues positively, fostering a more supportive and ethical workplace. I strongly recommend attending this workshop, as it will be a significant step toward personal and professional development.

Please let me know if you are interested, and I can arrange for our registrations.

Looking forward to your thoughts on this.

Best regards,

Rahul

Software Engineer

Email: da456gfe@gmail.com

In This Book

This book is a curated collection of previous years' Solved question papers for the *Professional Skills and Ethics* course offered by IGNOU. It serves as an essential tool for students preparing for exams by providing insight into the types of questions frequently asked and the patterns they follow. Designed to enhance your understanding of key topics, this resource encourages critical thinking and ethical decision-making. By practicing with these papers, you can reinforce your knowledge, identify areas for improvement, and build confidence, ensuring you are well-prepared to excel in your exams and your professional career.